To: Kai!
From Kristine

Sabertoothed cats of all ages have been found at La Brea in single groups. Some of the cats had injuries with signs of healing before being trapped in the asphalt. But how could cats hunt with serious injuries, like broken jaws and hips? They probably lived in family groups, whose members shared meals with them while they healed.

**FELINE FACT**
Some sabertoothed cats weighed 800 pounds!

Smilodon Saber...

# Big Cat Basics

Big cats are some of the most magnificent, awe-inspiring creatures on Earth. They're powerful and have extremely fast reactions! All cats, big and small, are primarily carnivores (meat-eaters). Cats have to be fast thinkers and fast killers. Their bodies are designed perfectly to find, chase, and kill prey.

Scientists believe that 37 cat species roam the Earth today. The nine biggest cats living are (in order of size, beginning with the smallest): the clouded leopard, Bornean clouded leopard, snow leopard, cheetah, leopard, puma, jaguar, lion, and tiger.

**FELINE FACT**
Cheetahs prey on a variety of animals, including thorny porcupines.

Snow Leopard

House Cat

## Bare Bones

A cat is a warm-blooded mammal with a four-chambered heart. Female cats give birth to live babies and produce milk to feed their young.

Cats have a protective skeleton with about 250 bones (compared to 206 in the human body). The skull is highly specialized for killing prey and devouring it quickly before other predators can steal it. The eye sockets (orbits) are large and round, allowing a wide field of vision.

Cats' jaws open extremely wide so their sharp canine teeth can deliver a killing bite to the neck. They swallow meat without chewing.

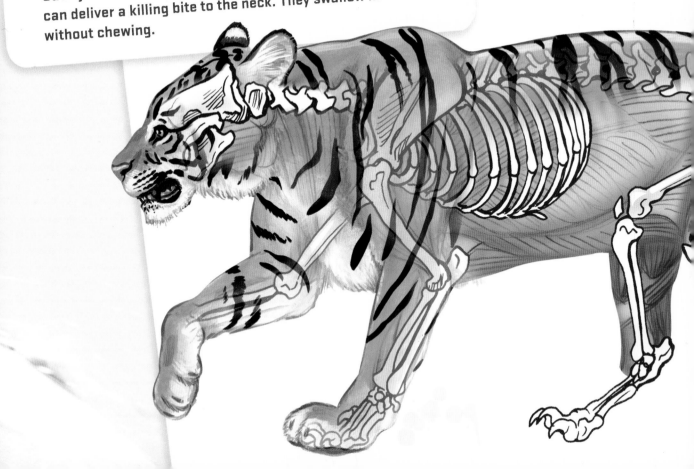

# Meet the Big Cats

## Clouded Leopards

live in the tropical rainforests and grasslands of Southeast Asia. These beautiful cats are called clouded leopards because the large spots on their fur resemble clouds. Their tails are the longest, in relation to body size, of any cat's tail.

## Cheetahs

live mostly in the grasslands of Africa. Their tan fur has solid black spots, and their sleek bodies weigh 100 to 170 pounds. While running, cheetahs can cover 22 feet in one stride! The fastest racehorse runs about 43 mph, while cheetahs can sprint up to 70 mph. They rely on speed to catch prey, and hunt during the day.

## Pumas

live in both freezing cold and scorching hot habitats. They roam from Canada through the United States to Central and South America. And since their hind legs are larger and more muscular than their front legs, pumas are great power-jumpers. This tan-colored cat is also called a mountain lion, cougar, or panther.

## Snow Leopards

live mainly in the high mountains of Central Asia. Smoky gray and blurred black markings provide the shy snow leopard with superb camouflage on cliffs and rocky slopes. The snow leopard's long tail helps with balance.

FELINE FACT
Pumas can jump 40 feet!

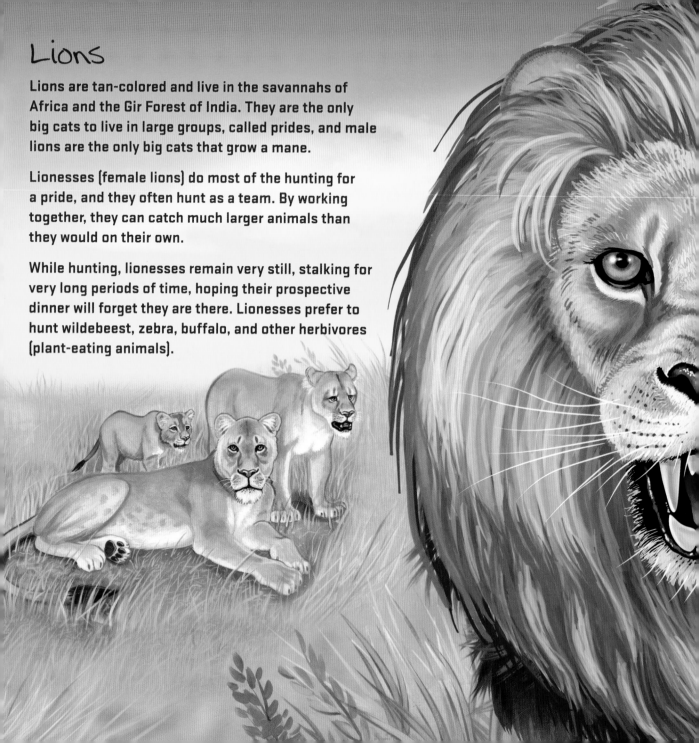

# Lions

Lions are tan-colored and live in the savannahs of Africa and the Gir Forest of India. They are the only big cats to live in large groups, called prides, and male lions are the only big cats that grow a mane.

Lionesses (female lions) do most of the hunting for a pride, and they often hunt as a team. By working together, they can catch much larger animals than they would on their own.

While hunting, lionesses remain very still, stalking for very long periods of time, hoping their prospective dinner will forget they are there. Lionesses prefer to hunt wildebeest, zebra, buffalo, and other herbivores (plant-eating animals).

After the prey is captured, male lions usually eat first. Sometimes males will also allow hungry cubs to nuzzle their way to first servings. During a single meal, a lion can eat as much as 100 pounds of meat, and a lioness can devour some 65 pounds.

FELINE FACT
A lion's thunderous roar can be heard up to five miles away!

# Meet the Big Cats

## Leopards

live in the forests, grasslands, and deserts of Africa and Asia. Their dark, flower-shaped spots, called rosettes, have solid edges and no dots in the center. They are able to run in bursts of speed just under 40 mph and leap 20 feet forward in a single bound!

Leopards look a lot like jaguars. Jaguars, however, are stockier and heavier, with shorter, thicker tails. Jaguars also have rosettes with irregular, broken borders, and, often, spots in the center.

**FELINE FACT**
Each cat's striped or spotted fur pattern is unique, like a human fingerprint.

## Jaguars

mainly live in the rainforests, woodlands, swamps, and deserts of Central and South America, but they can be found in arid regions of the southern United States. Unlike most big cats, the jaguar loves water. It hunts mostly on the ground at night, but it sometimes climbs trees and pounces on prey from above. Jaguars also hunt for fish, caimans, and crocodiles.

## Lions

can run the length of a 100-yard football field in six seconds! At two years old, a male lion begins to grow a mane around his neck. This mane can be nine inches long and is thought to protect the lion, to intimidate rivals, and to attract female mates.

## Tigers

What's black and white and orange all over? Tigers! (White tigers rarely occur in the wild; those in captivity are usually the result of inbreeding.) Different subspecies of tigers live in the jungles of Indonesia and snowy areas of Russia. A tigress has an average of three to four cubs.

# Super Senses

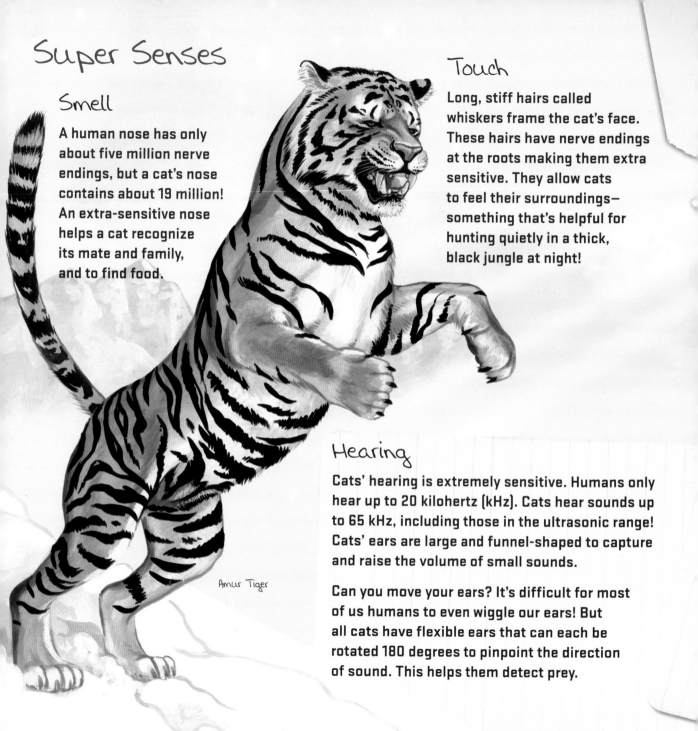

## Smell

A human nose has only about five million nerve endings, but a cat's nose contains about 19 million! An extra-sensitive nose helps a cat recognize its mate and family, and to find food.

## Touch

Long, stiff hairs called whiskers frame the cat's face. These hairs have nerve endings at the roots making them extra sensitive. They allow cats to feel their surroundings—something that's helpful for hunting quietly in a thick, black jungle at night!

Amur Tiger

## Hearing

Cats' hearing is extremely sensitive. Humans only hear up to 20 kilohertz (kHz). Cats hear sounds up to 65 kHz, including those in the ultrasonic range! Cats' ears are large and funnel-shaped to capture and raise the volume of small sounds.

Can you move your ears? It's difficult for most of us humans to even wiggle our ears! But all cats have flexible ears that can each be rotated 180 degrees to pinpoint the direction of sound. This helps them detect prey.